FREEMAN

Through the Water

Brooke Neal Freeman

ISBN 978-1-0980-6241-5 (paperback)
ISBN 978-1-0980-6242-2 (digital)

Christian Faith Publishing, Inc.
832 Park Avenue
Meadville, PA 16335
www.christianfaithpublishing.com

Printed in the United States of America

This book is to give God the glory. I tell my story to praise Him!

God gave my husband the physical strength and determination to hold fast. God sent his supernatural peace to me and allowed us to pray. He saved us!

To my parents, I am so thankful and proud you two are mine, my prayer warriors, the people who taught me how to pray.

To the US Coast Guard, for rerouting a plane for us and sending a ship to our rescue; God bless you.

To the Word Church and Rosewood First Baptist Church, both of Goldsboro, for all your crucial prayers on a Sunday morning, in a desperate hour, on July 23, 2017; thank you!

My life is forever changed.

When you go through deep waters, I will be with you.
When you go through rivers of difficulty, you will not drown.
When you walk through the fire of oppression,
you will not be burned up; the flames will not consume you.

—Isaiah 43:2, Holy Bible, New Living Translation

Preface

I pray this book is a blessing to all who pick it up, choose to read it, and share our miracle by word of mouth. I hope our story encourages you and makes you want to talk about God and all the things He has done, is capable of doing, and will do! Do not be afraid to speak what God has done and is doing for you. You never know who needs to hear your faith spoken out loud. I believe you can put God in anything, and you should put Him in everything!

I am a Christian. When our rescue occurred, I had recently graduated from Campbell University with a bachelor's degree in social work. I had just started graduate school at Edinboro University to obtain a master's in social work. I was a college cheerleader, and I truly believe being a cheerleader has been my role my whole life. I can be loud and competitive, and I enjoy getting everyone involved to have a good time. More importantly, I want to do God's work, to help and love people. I am an outdoorsy girl, love adventure, and believe I am closer to God while enjoying His creation. I am married to the man of my dreams, and I know God made him just for me. I would choose him all over again.

The focus of my master's program has been trauma. I chose this program many months before my friends and I were lost at sea. I believe God ordained this for me for many reasons; also, He knew I would need this knowledge for my own healing. I have seen many people that I love go through extremely traumatic experiences. Since beginning graduate school studies, I have found it *impossible* to stop thinking about surviving having been stranded in the ocean!

I want to give God the glory! I listen to K-Love and His radio stations 24/7. I want to stay in His presence. I want to be led by His Spirit now more than ever. I want to know more of the gospel. For weeks, I prayed about the emotions that I feel daily, that God would remove them out of my spirit. Often, I could not even talk without crying. The more I learned about trauma theories and how trauma affects people differently, the more I could heal and apply new knowledge to myself. I applied our trauma and how my friends and I reacted, and are still reacting to, our boat capsizing in the ocean.

That day in the ocean, I had a supernatural hope, in Jesus alone. I truly believe He had already arranged to have a US Coast Guard plane in the air for us. All five of us were, and are, *resilient* in different ways. Each of us has grown from this experience. "I know the plans I have for you," declares the Lord, "plans to prosper you and not to harm you, plans to give you a *hope* and a *future*."

My husband, Kenneth, is almost seven feet tall, and he is very handsome and muscular looking. He has been given the nickname "gentle giant" because he is so kind and respectful, always loving, even though he's pretty large. He played a bit of college football at East Carolina University and decided to join the ROTC while getting his bachelor's degree in criminal justice. Kenneth didn't end up going into the military as he had planned. God has mind-blowing ways to work things out exactly as He has planned; we had totally different plans for ourselves. I think Kenneth is smarter than me when it comes to classwork, and he has better hair than me. I hope our future kids are good at math like he is and have his thick locks. He loves to hunt and fish; he is a natural outdoorsman. I love and cherish all the times we spend together in nature. I was *obsessed* with *Duck Dynasty* a few years back; yes, I got my Phil Robertson! Kenneth is a Christian, and he has grown so much in his faith since July 23, 2017. Since our survival, we have spoken at a few local churches, and it is a dream come true to share the gospel and encourage others with my husband.

Kenneth and I have two dogs. We live in the middle of a farm, in an old house we restored with the help of my family. We partake in working on fixer-uppers with my family in our spare time. My parents were pretty much Chip and Joanna Gaines before *Fixer Upper* was a thing! Though we do not own the surrounding farm, we truly enjoy seeing the sunrises and sunsets, and our dogs love running the path.

We try to keep life pretty simple. We enjoy grilling out on weekends with family and close friends at "the camp." In the winter, we make s'mores. Warm weekends are often spent at the coast. We enjoy fishing, shelling, water sports, and days spent on the boat with people we love.

Before our experience in the ocean, some of the most mentally and physically challenging things I have faced in my lifetime have been coping with different family health circumstances, going through a few breakups while growing up, dealing with drama that came with being a college cheerleader, and my 9-month old kitten being hit by a car. Honestly, I know I am very blessed, and I have always been.

I truly believe I have been protected by many generations of prayer warriors in my family bloodline that came before me, and for that I am so thankful. I pray for the generations that will come after me. With that being said, I just recently realized how much *more* God has for me than the daily routine! Before our rescue, it was easy to be caught up in a daily routine consisting of work, school, church, and a few fun activities every weekend.

They say, "To whom much is given, much is expected." I realized I need to stop sitting around and *write* this book! It was time for me to stop making excuses and tell anyone who needs to know about *my miracle*!

If you feel like God is calling you to do something, stop putting it off! It's for His Glory and your good!

Speaking Out Your Faith

The father of one of my best friends was recently diagnosed with cancer. A later stage of cancer. He underwent chemo, radiation, and surgery. He battled daily with the help of God's strength. I say God's strength because he kept getting stronger as his treatment continued; as he faced more chemo. He gained weight; he even changed the way he dressed. There was a noticeable difference. My best friend did not accept the defeating news from all his doctors. She simply drew closer to God. She kept telling people in the community how God was going to heal her father. She couldn't keep quiet about what she knew God was doing! She continually spoke her miracle into existence, in Jesus's name. My father and "my" Linda went and prayed with him regularly. My friend's father leaned in to God, giving him a new joy and a purpose of witness.

I believe prayer changes things. In my lifetime, I have seen my parents stand on prayer when their lives were like a hurricane, unable to catch anything, but they stood on His Word. I can hear my mother saying, "I have to trust God." I believe we need to ask God for more miracles! What can God *not* do?

Recently, many in my hometown, people I did not expect to hear God speak through, have pointed out to me, "You need to write a book," "This story needs to be made into a movie," "Nicholas Sparks would love to have a story like yours." *Wow*. God wants to use little ole me to further His kingdom with the miracle He gave me and my friends! God pulled me and my friends out of the middle of the ocean! If He can do this for *me*, He can do *anything* for *you*. I am sure there are many who did not think I would be writing a book! A book to glorify *God*. But God!

I thank God I am able to tell you this story. I hope it blesses you and gives you the desire to make *sure*, in the wise words of Tim McGraw, you "live like you were dying." I have often heard these sayings: "You never know when it's your time" and "YOLO." YOLO became a popular slang when I was in high school—*you only live once* (on earth anyway)!

With both these sayings in mind, I also reflect on Francis Chan's famous rope illustration. If you don't know what I'm talking about, take the time to YouTube it right now! This illustration was once a game changer for me. Francis Chan said,

> Pretend this rope just goes on forever... Imagine that this rope is a timeline of your existence... You've got a few short years here on earth, and then you've got all of eternity somewhere else. This is your existence... It's crazy to me because the Bible teaches that what I do during this little part determines how I'm going to exist for millions and millions and millions of years forever. And so why would I spend this little part trying to make myself as comfortable as possible, enjoying myself as much as I can? ...We get one chance at this life on earth, and it can end at any second, for any of us. We've got one chance at this, and then comes eternity... People look at some of my decisions and say, Oh, you're so stupid because that's going to really affect this! ...I go, No, you're stupid, because it's going to affect all of this! I look at the way people live their earthly life, and I go, Wow! That is so crazy! (Chan, 2014).

It is my prayer that you know that you know, where you are going if you do not live to see tomorrow. And if you do, that you choose to muster the courage to share your testimony too. You never know who needs to hear your faith spoken out.

I know, that I know, God is the only reason my friends and I made it out of the ocean on July 23, 2017. He is not done writing our story. He can use what we went through for His Glory. God uses those who want to be used by Him, who are willing to be used.

This is my testimony.

My Childhood

The younger me went to church three times a week. I grew up in the church my Dad grew up in, on the corner, at the main traffic light in the Rosewood community. Three generations sat on that same church pew many Sundays of my life. My grandparents were long-time members at Rosewood First Baptist.

My grandmother, and my parents, help out with the local homeless shelter, the House of Fordham. Our family sometimes goes to the church affiliated with the shelter, the Word Church, where a family friend is the pastor. Linda Burroughs is my role model, to say the least. She started the shelter in 1986, after God gave her the vision to serve the community in this way. A friend to my grandmother and parents, as well as my husband and myself, Mrs. Linda loves like Jesus does. She is "famous" in my small town, and she knows the Word. She can *pray* and isn't ashamed to pour it out anywhere, for anyone. Both my parents were raised in Rosewood and have lived here most of their lives, except when they went off to college at East Carolina University. Everyone knows my parents are praying people, and this is something I am most proud of. I am proud of the way my parents raised me, and the standards they held me to.

When people asked me to give my testimony, growing up, in youth group, I never really felt like I had one. I think that was God's protection and mercy, from those prayer warriors before me in my family! I chose to get saved at a young age, and thankfully, I just couldn't narrow down a few pivotal moments of life into a testimony.

My dad, with God's help, faced cancer when I was very young; my parents raised me on the Word and prayer. I don't ever really remember not knowing Jesus. I *once* tried to preach at "youth Sunday" and still, six years later, in my mind recall that day as the most embarrassing time of my life. *But* I got up there; I think that's something!

Being stranded in the ocean with one of my lifelong best friends makes me want to tell you a little bit more about my childhood. I had a wonderful childhood! I grew up about two hours from the coast in a little country farm community. We would head to the beach or the lake almost every weekend. I had a lot of neighborhood friends, and a large extended family that lived just a few miles down the road in each direction. I have fond memories playing outside with my mom, dad, sister, and all the kids in my neighborhood! Growing up, I always enjoyed God's creations. I have happy memories of planting a garden with Mom, taking care of bunnies and goats, playing every sport with my dad as the coach, riding horses with my sister, playing flashlight tag with the neighborhood kids, swinging on our tire swing, having pool parties, eating blueberries right off the bushes in the yard, learning water sports, riding ATVs, and going camping somewhere every summer! I will always cherish my childhood memories.

My best friends were Dayton and Payton Meadows, two of the six kids from next door. Payton is about four years younger than me. I remember playing with her like she was my baby doll when she was a small child. Payton and I became the very best of friends when we tried out for a competitive cheerleading team together, about twelve years ago now.

Payton and I had always been good friends, but from competitive cheerleading years forward, she and I were inseparable and had an alliance to one another. Payton was always mature for her age—in decision-making, looks—and she was always advanced in school. Dayton was my age. We played together almost every day as children. When Dayton and I both started playing sports in middle school, it was no longer "cool" to have a best friend of the other sex, and Dayton and I grew apart. When we were growing up, my sister Olivia would hang out with Payton and Dayton's older sisters, Chandra and Haile. Our older siblings, all three, were around the same age. Haile would often include Payton and me, Haile being the youngest of the three older siblings. She would give us "makeovers" and "spot" us learning how to do backflips. Also, she loved to play house and pretend she was our "mom" and take care of us. As children, we shared so many memories together that today all of us kids still choose to be more like family. I choose to believe God knew we would need each other.

High School Fling

In 2011, I was playing varsity volleyball at my high school; I was a sophomore. A tall middle schooler named Lillian had transferred to my school, and our coach pulled her up to practice and dress out on the varsity team. Her brother would come "watch her play" even though she sat on the bench. He kept coming back. Lillian was a great player when she played; she was just very young at the time. Kenneth did not transfer with his sister because our school did not have a football team, and he did not want to miss any college football scholarship opportunities. Anyway, Kenneth kept coming back to our volleyball games, and all the girls noticed! I mean, he was almost seven feet tall.

The Wayne Regional Agricultural Fair rolled around the end of September. I was at the fair with some of my closest friends, one being Queen of the Fair that year. So of course, we had to go to the fair as often as possible; it was a social event each day. One of my friends saw the older brother of someone she was sort of "talking to." The older brother, who was at the fair with his friend group, dated a girl from our church. She and I cheered together, and our parents were friends. Her mother was my Sunday school teacher. Naturally, our circles merged; we stood talking on the "midway." Kenneth was walking around the fair with this group of his friends when our circles collided, and he said to me, "You play volleyball at Wayne Country Day. I've seen you at my sister's games." I acted like it was no big deal that he just said that he remembered seeing me play at his sister's volleyball games! Inside, I actually almost peed myself! I have no idea what I said back to him, but I guess it was something good, because later that week, he messaged me on Facebook asking for my number. I then texted all my friends, freaking out about it! He continued coming to sporting events at my school. I would go watch him play basketball at his high school too.

Kenneth remembers playing cards with my sister and her boyfriend in my parents' bonus room one weekend. He would come to hang out at my house with my family. I dragged him to the church affiliated with the House of Fordham homeless shelter, the Word Church, and he didn't get scared off. In fact, everyone loved him, and that kind of freaked me out! My friend, the pastor, Mrs. Linda, told me how much she liked Kenneth. I looked at her like she had eight heads when she said, "He's the one."

Kenneth would accompany me to gatherings when I needed a date, and he would invite me to places as well. He started talking about college football and the military after graduating from ECU. I wasn't too fond of the idea of marrying an officer in the military and moving away from my family. Honestly, I didn't think I could be in a relationship with a college football player. He went off to play football for ECU his freshman year. I remember him texting me and telling me he would make peanut butter sandwiches in the morning before his classes; he would eat sandwiches while walking to the next class. I went to see him for Halloween, and I remember thinking, *I'm never coming here again.* He sent me flowers for my birthday in January, but our friendship fizzled out before February of 2012. Nothing really happened for us to "stop talking." We kept occasional contact for a year or so after that. Once in a blue moon, we would like one of each other's photos on social media. We didn't talk often, and we just went our separate ways. He adjusted to the college life, and I continued with my life back home.

We both started dating other people and, somehow along the way, did not keep up with one another on social media. We lost each other's numbers because of getting new phones and eventually lost contact completely because of "unfriending" each other on social media when we got in more "serious" relationships. His sister and I remained friends; we went to a small school where both of us only had twenty to thirty people in our graduating classes. His sister was always a ray of sunshine—a fourwheelin', fishin', down-to-earth, sweet, life-living girl. I would see his parents at her school events, and we would speak, and things just went on as what seemed normal. There were really no hurt feelings. If he came to see his sister play while he was on a break, we would sometimes speak depending on whom either of us was with.

Falling for Kenneth, the Man Who Is Now My Husband

Five years later, in 2016, I was home from college on summer break after just completing my junior year. Our paths happened to cross again. I was a student athlete with required daily workouts from a weight trainer. I was going to the YMCA regularly when I happened to bump into Kenneth in the weight room. He wasn't a regular face at the YMCA, at that time of day anyway. I noticed he was wearing a shirt honoring his best friend's brother. It read, "Lift for Lynch." His best friend's brother had recently died in a hunting accident. That best friend was one of the guys he was at the fair with five years ago. They had been friends forever, I remembered. I had heard all about the accident. It was devastating for our community. It was all over social media. I asked about his best friend and his friend's family, and we caught up for a few minutes about how everyone was coping. I kept up with the brother's girlfriend, who was dealing with the tragic loss. I had cheered with her for a few years.

We made small talk about our own lives. Kenneth told me he did not end up being able to go into the military; he had tried multiple times for every branch. When he could not get in, it was life altering for him. Kenneth was in ROTC in college after getting hurt playing football his freshman year. He had serious plans, for several years, that he would go into the military after graduating. He was turned away because of the curvature of his spine; he has scoliosis. Things didn't work out the way he had planned.

Kenneth was living with his parents and was hog-farming for a local company where his father farmed turkeys as well. He had dated a girl most of the time he was in college, and things didn't work out between them. He asked if I was in a serious relationship. I told him how I had been, and it had just ended abruptly. We exchanged numbers and added each other on Snapchat standing right there in the weight room at the Goldsboro YMCA! We laughed about how we should get together and then went on with our days. He was leaving the gym, and I was getting started with my workout.

After my workout, I stopped by my dad's office; he was busy working. I was talking, and he as working hard as he could. I said to my dad, "I'm thinking about hanging out with Kenneth Freeman again. What do you think?" He said something along the lines of "Okay, fine," and continued working. He didn't realize that was his moment to speak or forever hold his peace!

The next day, Kenneth Snapchatted me a photo of a brand-new sports car he drove off the lot. He wrote "Guess what" on a selfie, then sent another photo of his new car and wrote on the photo "Check it out." Somehow, my fingers typed the words "We should hang out" on a selfie and sent it back to him.

Kenneth called me a few minutes later and invited me, and a few of my girlfriends, to Atlantic Beach for the weekend, to his cousin's beach house. It was a Monday. I was thinking, *How will I ever make it to the weekend!* Kenneth, his cousin, and their guy friends were going, and they pretty much had the mind-set of the more the merrier. We girls rolled in Saturday morning and grabbed some sunglasses from the Wings right by his cousin's house, and we took off on their pontoon boat! We spent all day on the water singing "Somewhere on a Beach" by Dierks Bentley. We met up with a slew of young people on an island and ended up getting on a houseboat with a mutual friend. We all danced on the top floor of the houseboat. It was someone's birthday party, but none of us knew her! Kenneth danced with me and then handed me off to another guy wanting a dance. Kenneth grabbed another girl, and they spun around. I couldn't tell you whom I was dancing with because I was just watching Kenneth dance with another girl. One of my girlfriends found a Hula-Hoop somewhere, and we started Hula-Hooping. Someone was flying a drone over all the boats for a social media post of the island party. We girls posed to take cute pictures to post on Instagram and jumped off the upper deck, hand in hand, making Boomerang videos all afternoon.

We somehow made it home right before dark, showered, and got ready to go downtown to Morehead for food and more fun. We ate dinner and danced on the boat dock that evening to a cover band singing Chris Stapleton's "Tennessee Whiskey" on the Beaufort waterfront.

A few days later, Kenneth asked me to dinner at a steak house. He picked me up, but then I got into the driver's seat. I drove his car a hundred miles an hour down a backroad and lived to tell about it! I mean, I only went a hundred for about three seconds, Mom!

Kenneth had been working every other weekend until this point on the hog farm. When we first started hanging out, I was really bummed about this. I have always spent my summers on the water! I honestly thought to myself, *How are we going to date if he has to work weekends all summer?*

As we started going on dates more regularly, my dad asked me if I had been praying for Kenneth. Sure, I had been praying for "the man God had for me" my whole life, but I had not started praying for Kenneth since we had been going on dates. I felt like it was God sending me a message, and so did Kenneth, because as soon as I started really praying for him, he got a promotion; he was allowed weekends off. I give God the glory for that!

We quickly started spending all our time together. Summer weekends were at Topsail Island, at my parents' beach house, which we call the Hidden Safari Beach Shack. We had our friends come as often as possible. We went fishing, learned new water sport tricks, and cooked dinner on the grill. We would wake up when the sun came up and stay up half the night.

Back at home, Kenneth and I enjoyed evenings hanging out with friends, riding his parents' side-by-side, having a fire at the "man cave," and so on. Somehow, he would make it to the farm every day by 5:00 a.m. and still do a great job.

Kenneth's farm would earn the statistic of the "highest production rate" of baby pigs out of all the hog farmers he would "compete" with almost every month. I would jokingly tell him the job was just too easy for him. Kenneth would tell me about studying pig semen under the microscope, doing C-sections on the pigs, seeing the ultrasounds, doing different jobs on the tractor, and striving to keep all the pigs healthy and producing.

August approached so quickly! Cheerleading drew me back to Campbell more and more for mandatory twenty-hour weekend camps and practices. School would be starting, and football season was approaching. We would plan for any second we could see each other, when he was off work and I wasn't in class or at practice or cheering at a game. Kenneth would come to every game. He was at Campbell if I couldn't come home. Everyone would ask Kenneth, "Why don't you play football?" or make jokes about how our football team really needed him.

I would often have Wednesdays off from practice, and I'd only have morning classes. Kenneth and I would try to spend most of the day together Wednesday, messing around in the woods with trail cameras, scouting land for new places to hunt, playing on the lake his parents live on, or just going to the gym and to dinner.

Kenneth talked to me about going to the beach on an upcoming Wednesday, September 28, 2016. I had seen an *Our State* magazine issue with wild horses featured a few months prior, and Kenneth's dad had a boat on the lift at Olde Towne Yacht Club, Radio Island, at his relative's condo. I had mentioned that I wanted to see the horses. I told Kenneth a few times, "Take me on your dad's boat to see those horses!" About a week before, Kenneth told me that he worked it out to take me! He suggested we dress up and take some cute pics with those horses in the background and go to the lighthouse. This was my love language! I was so excited about our upcoming adventurous date. I had just ordered a new Lilly dress from the "end of the after-party sale" and knew exactly what I was going to wear.

My mom packed an overnight bag for me that Wednesday morning; I found that very unusual. I actually don't remember another time she ever has done this since I was a child. I remember looking at her, while I was standing there in her kitchen wearing my new light-blue Lilly dress and Jack Rogers sandals, and saying, "We're coming back tonight!" I sort of questioned why she was handing me a bag she had packed for me. I didn't look inside, and I didn't take the bag.

Kenneth arrived and we headed out. I don't remember much about leaving my parents' house. Maybe I ran back upstairs to my room to get something I left. Maybe I ran to the back of the house to tell my dad bye. But somehow the bag my mother packed for me got into Kenneth's car. I saw my bag in the back seat of his car at some point on the way to the beach, and I rolled my eyes and laughed to myself. A few seconds after seeing it, *it* hit me! *Is Kenneth about to propose? Why are we so dressed up on a Wednesday? I should have gotten my nails done! Normally, we'd be messing around in T-shirts right now!* We stopped to get gas, and Kenneth got out of the car. I called my mom and said, "Why am I so dressed up on a Wednesday? Is Kenneth about to propose to me?" And she actually didn't crack, or let on, or anything.

A few hours later, we were on the boat dock with a photographer "Kenneth knew," who told me he was going to update his website. Kenneth told him he could take pics of us for advertisement purposes. I was so excited about this and asked him how we would be able to get the photos. He stated he guessed I could just screenshot them off his page. I was disappointed by this remark and went on rambling about the quality of the photos if I were to screenshot them. If I could get him to e-mail them to us, I would gladly pay him for them! I was actually a bit annoyed by his answer, but we were on the sea, and the sun was shining.

We found the horses almost immediately! It was just like a dream, even better than the photographs in the *Our State* magazine, I thought. Kenneth laughed in disbelief and amazement. Earlier that day on the way he had said, "I hope we can find them," and I answered with something along the lines of "Things just happen for us that don't happen for most people." The horses were swimming in the water beside the boat, and one was standing on a sandbar with the lighthouse in the background. I couldn't have placed them any more perfectly if I had been able to pose them myself!

I never suspected that Kenneth was paying this photographer, that these photos weren't really to update the photographer's website! I mean, crazy, wonderful things would just happen to us, often! The horse, for example—we had no control over that. That was God.

We arrived at Cape Lookout and walked all over, taking pictures. I asked Kenneth, "Why are you acting so uptight?" And he said, "What are you talking about?" Then, right when we were going to head back to the boat to end a wonderful day adventuring all over Cape Lookout and seeing the horses, Kenneth got down on one knee and choked up while asking me to marry him! <u>I wish I had written down, right then, how he asked. All I know is, I answered, "*finally!*" and threw my arms around him!</u> He really tried to convince me that the ring went on my right hand too. We all three died laughing when the photographer didn't know either! I was all smiles and laughs! That evening, we walked around downtown Beaufort as the sun was setting; enjoying the beautiful views and the boats docked on North Carolina's historic coast.

After we got engaged, we came home to celebrate with our immediate family. Next, we took off on a plane to Oxford, Mississippi, where Payton was a freshman at Ole Miss. She and my parents knew about the proposal ahead of time, and Kenneth had coordinated the trip to see her for the weekend. It was Payton's birthday weekend. We had promised her a birthday visit back in the summer, and now she could help us celebrate!

We set our wedding date and planned for August 5, 2017. This date would have me graduated, and our friends would not have left for fall college semesters yet. And very importantly, we would still have our suntans. By "plan" I mean we took dance lessons, and my mom called all the shots. I showed her things I liked on Pinterest. She was my wedding planner. The best wedding planner. We were too in love to worry about little details. We were getting married! I snagged a $50 wedding dress from a local thrift store, and a dear family friend helped me make it "perfect" for me. I couldn't spend too much time shopping because I just wanted to be adventuring with Kenneth.

While we were engaged for almost a year, my parents helped flip us a white farmhouse. By the end of it, the house had a phenomenal porch, a breathtaking all-white kitchen with black countertops, soft tan walls, all-white trim. We saved the old hardwood floors throughout the house and refinished them. We even transformed the falling-down back porch into a master bathroom accessed through a sliding barn door off the master bedroom. People call my dad weekly, still, asking how much money it would take for him to sell that house. We lived there about a year. We call it our "honeymoon house." When my parents purchased the fixer-upper, they didn't know we'd want to live there, but it was truly a dream come true! I didn't know how wonderful it would be at the time. every time I pass by, I think to myself, *I loved that place*. I planted as many flowers as I could, and Kenneth was in the swamp out back almost every day. Just a few days before being rescued by the USCG, we installed a huge American flag in the front yard. When we moved, the flag went with us!

My little cousin Martin took a real liking to Kenneth, and they immediately formed a bond like brothers. Martin was about to turn fourteen when Kenneth came into the picture. Any time he knew we were doing something outdoors and he didn't have school, Martin was dying to tag along. Martin's family lived right around the corner.

Kenneth and I spent every minute we could together playing outside! He would help me garden, or I would be with him in the swamp. He even humored me when I wanted a greenhouse made with PVC pipe, as seen on Pinterest! We went adventuring everywhere we could think of. We visited the Outer Banks and saw a few more North Carolina lighthouses and flew in a small plane over Kill Devil Hills. We went hiking all over the North Carolina mountains and saw so many beautiful waterfalls. We pulled a twenty-year-old pop-up camper that the Meadows family gave us as an engagement gift. They had not used it for years. They knew we were young and in love and would use it! It did not have a bathroom, sink, heater, air-conditioning, or anything to cook in. It had a few ratholes in it, which we repaired with duct tape, and it was *perfect*! We were thrilled! Airbnbs had nothing on us and our pop-up.

Life seemed new and exciting with Kenneth! I know God sent him to me, not just because we have fun together, but because God knew I needed him and we would make an amazing team. Together, we can move mountains. When we first fell in love, we would jokingly say, "We've got the world!" Everywhere we went, we felt loved, accepted, and welcomed. We truly felt like we had everything. We felt like God was blessing us continually. We had no idea, and still have no idea, what *all* God will do. Life together was, and still is, an adventure!

Miracles

Payton recently sent me a sermon by Lee Strobel, a former atheist who chose to get saved while trying to disprove miracles. Isn't that like God? He addresses the true meaning of a *miracle*. He quoted Richard Purtill, who defines a miracle as this: "A miracle is an event brought about by the power of God that is a temporary exception to the ordinary course of nature for the purpose of showing that God has acted in history (Strobel, 2018)." Strobel also mentions a quote from Skeptics magazine that claims, "Only the uneducated and uncivilized believe in miracles" (Strobel, 2018). Yet, scientifically trained, well-educated persons believe in miracles; a recent poll taken of physicians in the U.S. revealed 55% of them reported having witnessed a miracle (Strobel, 2018). In this national poll, conducted by *HCD Research* and the *Louis Finkelstein Institute for Religious and Social Studies of the Jewish Theological Seminary,* a full 74% of physicians reported their belief in miracles (Bishop, 2015)"

June 2017

In June of 2017, our wedding was only a few weeks away! Kenneth, my fiancé (!), and I planned to go fishing with Haile Meadows and her boyfriend, Alex. Alex was the proud new owner of a fishing boat, so naturally, he was fishing somewhere every weekend. He was over the moon about his "new" boat. The boat was cleaned up good, and it ran! It had been well-kept by the older gentleman Alex purchased it from. It had a small cabin, which was perfect for storing our fishing gear and other boating necessities, like huge beach bags full of everything we could possibly need. I grew up on the water and didn't question if the boat was safe. It looked and sounded like a day of fun in the sun, and I just didn't think of questioning it. Growing up boating with my family, my father kept everything shipshape. He could pass a boat inspection any day. I never had to think about having all the necessities, like enough life jackets, a fire extinguisher, and so on, because my father had already thought of them for us. I am guessing Alex's new boat was at least fifteen or maybe even twenty years old. I am unclear on the make and model of this boat.

Super early that morning, Kenneth and Alex woke up to put the boat in at the Crutchfield Avenue private boat ramp by my grandmother's beach house. The sign reads, "Heaven is a little closer in a home by the sea." I spent my summers growing up on "top secret" Topsail Island. I claimed to be a local, for part of the year anyway. Haile and I slept at my parents' house, just a few streets over, on Mermaid Lane. We had prepared for this fishing trip the night before with a late run to the grocery store on the island, at the good ole IGA. Trying to get all the sleep possible, we were planning on going "fishing" with the guys, even though we didn't know exactly how much fishing we would actually do. We would eat, tan, and talk! Haile and I were along for the ride, to get a suntan and take Instagram photos with the fish! We were a dream team support squad equipped with a Nikon, GoPro and cell phones, to properly document the day. Maybe we would get the chance to reel a few in, if the guys really got into 'em!

The guys let us sleep until the last possible minute. They had the boat in the water and tied to the dock. All their fishing gear and tackle ready and on the boat, they busted into the house right at the crack of dawn. The boys came into the house hollering with excitement, "Come on! We're going fishing!" "Let's go!" "Get up!" They yelled to wake us as they went into the kitchen to fill a cooler with ice and foods we prepared the night before. Peanut butter and jelly sandwiches, chocolate chip cookies, fresh-cut fruits, and plenty of Gatorade.

I stumbled through the living room half-asleep and headed to the bathroom since Haile had gone into my bathroom. As I walked across the room with bed head, half asleep, I mumbled, "I had a dream that we caught a big blueish-green fish," and I held my arms out to show how big the fish was. I sleepily told the guys that, in my dream, Kenneth had to help me hold the fish; I couldn't even hold it by myself! The guys didn't pay me much mind. I acted out how Kenneth and I were holding the fish together in my dream. I squatted down into an athletic stance and motioned that Kenneth was behind my back helping me hold the fish by its head and tail fin horizontally, posing for a photo. I giggled and was joyous about the dream I had just had. I headed into the bathroom as Alex and Kenneth laughed and hurried me along.

I came out of the bathroom, continuing to talk excitedly about our fishing trip and the dream I had just had. Kenneth showed me photos on Google, images of a mahi-mahi, and asked if this was the fish from my dream. I excitedly agreed that was the fish from my dream! I had never gone deep-sea fishing. Alex and Kenneth proceeded to tell me there was no way we could catch a fish that I dreamed of; we were only going a mile out, and it wasn't the time of year for mahi-mahi. They laughed harmlessly at me, explaining to me we would be catching Spanish mackerel. I jokingly, but confidently, assured them we were going to catch the fish from my dream! Alex and Kenneth were experienced deep-sea fishermen. They explained to me it wasn't the right time of year for mahi-mahi, but maybe later in the year and farther out in the ocean. Kenneth grew up fishing on his uncle's sixty-eight-foot "Sea Hag" out of Morehead City. Alex grew up fishing all over with his father. The guys reassured me we would be catching Spanish mackerel using live menhaden as bait. We all laughed as I walked through the living room in my pajamas back to my room to get my bathing suit on. Haile proceeded to harmlessly poke fun by telling me about a coworker of hers that believes that all her dreams have meanings and that she can interpret dreams. I had never dreamed about something and then had it actually come to pass that I was aware of. I knew little about dreams and their meanings. I did believe dreams could be interpreted. Years ago, I dreamed I was chasing a turtle, and I asked my friend what she thought about it. Mrs. Linda laughed and told me I was chasing something I was never going to catch, not because I wasn't fast enough, but because I wasn't supposed to catch it. Whatever I was chasing was not for me!

I was not offended by my friends making fun of my dream at all. I just wondered in the back of my mind, *Could this mean something?* I gave little thought to my dream as I was getting ready for the day. I told Kenneth, Haile, and Alex about it, and that was that. Everyone believed I had the dream; just no one believed it was actually going to happen. Kenneth and Alex had basically said that the season and the conditions, in the natural, simply weren't in my favor.

Haile and I threw on our bikinis, a little bit of makeup, and our cover-ups. Everyone proceeded to the dock. In just minutes, we were off, we headed into the sloughs down from the Harbor Village Marina, about a ten-minute boat ride from the house. Kenneth and I had found a "good bait spot" a few weeks prior. The good bait spot was a shallow canal hidden way back in the marsh of Hampstead. There was a subdivision sign in the marsh, and we thought that was just too cool. Sometimes the tide gets so low you can't get a boat in there at all. Apparently, those baitfish like hiding in there like that.

At our bait spot, Kenneth threw the cast net and Alex drove. It's a real task chasing down baitfish in such shallow water, maneuvering the boat at such a slow speed in a narrow area and not getting beached. I sat back and caught up with Haile. This was a nice break for me, because normally, when Kenneth and I go fishing, he will throw the cast net and I will (try and) be the captain. Thankfully, this time Alex was the captain, and I got to be a passenger, since we were on Alex's boat! Haile and I were talking and carrying on, enjoying being on the water and relaxing. The boys chased the ripples in the water that indicated fish, and shortly, we had enough baitfish to head out to sea. Just enough mullet and menhaden for bait. We couldn't waste any more daylight inshore. I thought nothing of the bait we caught. I was just enjoying the beautiful day. We were headed out to sea. The inlet was about a ten-minute drive from where we were. Alex and Kenneth researched and planned our deep-see fishing destination to be over an artificial reef known as AR 360, just a couple of miles off the shore of Topsail Beach. Haile and Alex said, "We'll be right across from the pier!" They had fished this spot before.

I was a little nervous since this was my first time deep sea fishing. I stood up and held on to the side of the boat as we slammed through the inlet and out into sea. It seemed rough, but they told me as soon as we got past the breakers, it would be better. If I had not stood up, I believe I would have been thrown into the floor, thrown out of the boat, or broken my tailbone from slamming the seat so hard. Haile and Alex had been here fishing the few weekends before; they said Topsail Inlet is a rough inlet! The ocean seemed a lot calmer after we passed through the worst of the inlet. Alex drove us like he had been a captain his whole life; never did his childlike smile leave his face! He was clearly loving the fishing trip already, just the thrill of being on the water.

On our way out to the reef, we saw the most beautiful school of stingrays, swimming together. I cannot find words to describe their beauty as they flowed with the waves like a blanket connected. They did "the wave" in unison through the water. I had never seen such. Here's an iPhone photo that really doesn't come close to describing their beauty! If only you could see them in motion. PS: That's Topsail Island in the background.

When we reached the reef, we could still see the Topsail beach shoreline in the distance. It did look as if we were directly in front of the Jolly Roger Pier, just like Haile and Alex had said. The guys got the rods in the water and we began trolling over the reef. Alex put a balloon on one of the rods, a little trick his father had taught him. There were quite a few poles in the water with live menhaden bait on them. The guys jokingly put a mullet on one line for bait, just to give it a try, to "conserve" the "good bait." I overheard them say this and thought nothing of it.

Haile and I made our way to the front of the boat. We laid our towels out and positioned ourselves on the bow to get some sun, on top of the cabin of the boat. We spoke more about our siblings and our parents. We saw a huge sea turtle come to the surface of the water for just a second, not long enough to photograph it, but it was absolutely unbelievable! I wish I had a photo to show for it! Seriously, this day does not seem real looking back! I had previously only seen sea turtles at the Karen Beasley Sea Turtle Rescue and Rehabilitation Center. The Topsail Turtle Hospital rescues and cares for sick and injured sea turtles until they are healthy enough to be released back into the ocean. We were so thrilled to see the turtle, we said to each other that made it "worth it" going with the guys, just seeing the beauty of a school of stingrays swimming in unison and a huge sea turtle come to surface! I was really enjoying God's creation and praising Him. The day seemed unbelievable.

I remember singing in my head "Even If" by MercyMe, a song that had just made it big on the radio. I would listen to it on the treadmill in the mornings on repeat. It was my jam. It really built my faith and helped me pray through some things going on at that time in my life. It was such a worshipful morning on the water. Haile and I fell asleep in the sun, and the guys were in their own world.

We woke up to the guys screaming with excitement. There was a fish on the line! Kenneth grabbed the pole and began to fight the fish! The fishing line fiercely unwound at uncontrollable speed and made a loud whining. We could not contain our excitement! Haile and I ran down the sides of the boat from the bow to the floor. I grabbed the steering wheel and took over as captain. Alex grabbed the gaff. Haile dashed into the cabin, grabbed her GoPro, and began filming. Alex hovered over Kenneth with the gaff in anticipation. He encouraged him as he fought the fish. We all screamed as the fish jumped out of the water! *It was a mahi-mahi flipping in and out of the water and through the air!* God, it was beautiful! The colors were indescribable, colors only a deep-sea fisherman could understand. I had never seen this in my life! Haile screamed, "Your dream, dude, oh my God!" as the fish kept swimming fiercely, flipping and fighting, now closer to the boat. Kenneth yelled for Alex to get ready to gaff the fish. Kenneth led the fish to the boat for Alex to assist, and like a pro, he did. Kenneth reeled it right into Alex's gaffing reach. Alex and Kenneth performed like a team that had been training together for this moment their entire lives. Haile and I cheered our hearts out! I was so excited! I look like an absolute lunatic in the video I posted on YouTube! Alex raised the fish over his head still on the gaff! Kenneth's faced looked like he was in shock that we had caught it and gotten it in the boat successfully, and Haile had videoed the whole thing! Haile shouted, "Your dream, dude!" on film. Unbelievable, to say the least. We each posed for photos with the fish. We were in complete disbelief of what had just happened. I learned that day that as soon as the fish comes out of the water, it's colors immediately begin to fade. You literally cannot capture, or describe, the beauty unless you see it being reeled in.

After things calmed down, I lay on the front of the boat and wept with joy and wonder. I praised God. I could not figure out why He would do all these amazing things for us in one day. I laughed as I praised God and thought to myself, *Because He can!*

The guys put the line back into the water, and we continued trolling. We fished for at least five more hours and caught nothing. Haile was sunburned; she had fallen asleep without sunscreen. We decided to call it a day. This is a day I will always remember as one of the *best* days of my life.

When we returned to the beach house, we showed our fish off to everyone we knew on the island. Family and friends drove over to see our fish! Kenneth showed all the little kids the fish, and they all watched him cut it up like a science class dissection. We made dinner plans with the whole crowd to grill the fish! Everyone planned to bring something to add to the table. We uploaded the video to our computer and watched it multiple times! The joy it produced was continual, we couldn't stop watching it. I immediately shared it on my social media.

All the odds had been against us. It seemed to have been impossible for us to catch a mahi-mahi on mullet, out of season, a couple of miles offshore. My dream, however, was what really made it so unbelievable! I remember just praising and praying and asking God why He would show me, in a dream, the fish we would catch. I cried and laughed over and over; I felt like God was telling me, just because He could! He showed me his control over the ocean; He showed me in a loving, almost silly, way that He could do anything! He is *good*; He wants good for us. He increased my faith that day by showing me a fish in a dream and bringing it to pass. God prepared me for the next chapter of my life; I just did not understand it at the time. God strengthened me, purposefully, in preparation.

Moving in the Spirit

As an "early wedding gift," my parents purchased Kenneth a new cell phone. Kenneth would often run out of data at the end of the month and often could not even receive calls at the farm he worked on. Dad could add Kenneth to his business plan for much cheaper than the plan Kenneth had; he would get the newest iPhone at that time. My father is not frivolous, nor is my mother; they have both worked very hard all their lives and would not do such a thing if they had not really considered and prayed about it. It was a wonderful gift, and Kenneth and I were both super appreciative at the time. We did not realize how appreciative we would be. God had ordained this; I believe this gift was not by any other means. I believe my father was obedient to the Holy Spirit. I believe he did not know at the time the magnitude of this cell phone; he just knew to love Kenneth.

July 2017

Just a few short weeks later, two weekends before our wedding, Payton was finally home, so we all went out to dinner to celebrate. She had been everywhere doing mission work, volunteering, and seeing the world. She was finally home just for a little while before she had to go back to Ole Miss. We kept up on FaceTime and through texts; she was a sophomore at Ole Miss, studying hard to become a dentist. Over dinner, we heard stories about Young Life camp and her visits around the United States to new friends she made at school. Payton did not want to be stuck in our small town for too long. I had missed her so much all summer. I jokingly said we were going to the beach together the next day, to make up for the whole summer! Growing up, we spent many summer days together at Topsail Island. Most of my favorite memories growing up involve Payton.

At Texas Roadhouse, we ran into Payton's sister, Haile, and Alex, with Patrick, Alex's brother. Alex and Haile were celebrating his brother's birthday; the next day, Patrick would be 25. The guys cooked up a plan to continue Patrick's birthday celebration with a fishing trip the next day. Payton and I were beach bound; they couldn't stand the thought of us going to the coast without them! The excitement inside me grew; I wanted to go fishing too!

Just a couple weeks earlier, we experienced that amazing day fishing. One of the best days of my life. Payton wanted to go the beach the next day to lay out; I was dying to go fishing with the guys! I figured we could combine the two; we could lay out on the front of the boat like Haile and I had done. I told her how much fun we had; she had seen the video! We could catch some rays from the bow of the boat! She was skeptical, but I had become an expert in convincing her to do things (like leave the house after 9:30 p.m. to go get ice cream with boys; yes, I'm being serious!). Payton has always had a pretty level head on her shoulders. We headed to the beach, still unsure of exactly where we would soak up the sun the next day!

Payton, Kenneth, and I rode together; Alex and Patrick drove separately, pulling the boat. Payton and I had both hoped that Haile would come to the beach too. However, she was taking an antibiotic and could not be in the sun. Haile did not want to sit in the house all day. We got to the beach late. I woke up my passengers, just to zombie-walk to the bed and fall back asleep; I passed out myself.

The guys woke us up early, and we got ready in a hurry. I still remember Payton saying, "Are we really going with them?"

I urged her, "Come on. It'll be fun."

Like our previous fishing trip, the guys were up much earlier and had everything ready and the boat tied to the dock. I assume Payton just decided to go fishing because I wanted to; I peer-pressured her into going. We threw on our bikinis, cover-ups, and shoes and quickly packed a cooler and a bag. I specifically remembered grabbing my mom's biggest, softest, nicest beach towels. On the dock, we walked right past my family's boats on the lifts and got on Alex's boat. Alex and Patrick had brought the special rods and reels that had belonged to their recently deceased father. This was their seasoned "good luck" fishing gear. Someone untied the boat from the dock, and we headed out to get our baitfish! Like the last time, we went to our best bait spot. I remember snapping a photo of a beautiful heron; he was also fishing for baitfish that morning. I posted him on my Instagram story! I lost my phone in the ocean later on this day, so I have no other photos except the ones Kenneth took.

Payton and I posed for Kenneth to take pictures of us in our bikinis to post on Instagram. We talked the entire morning, about most of which I don't even remember. What stands out to me that I do remember was Payton telling me the statistics and how all the odds were against her getting into dental school out of state. She loved Mississippi and didn't want to move back to North Carolina for dental school but wasn't completely opposed to it. UNC was her first choice, if she decided to come back home. I went on about her being a straight A student, with all sorts of extracurricular activities to make her even more appealing, a sorority girl, and one of the most athletic people I have ever known. She is super well-rounded; I am so unsure how I got so lucky to have her as a best friend my whole life! Did I mention she got a perfect score on the SAT? I told her that the odds had always been against her success but that she should look where she is and see all that she has accomplished already! She smiled. Payton has always been determined. She showed me a guy on Instagram she was keeping up with still since school had let out. She told me about friends she was missing and was excited to see when she got back to school.

As we approached the inlet, I coached Payton that last time it was more comfortable to stand up. So we stood up and held on in an athletic stance so we wouldn't get slammed around going through the breakers. We were sprayed with water; my cover-up was drenched because of the angle of the waves splashing the boat. Payton commented on how rough it was. Every time we hit a big wave, the lid to the live well flapped open; water and baitfish sloshed out, and then the lid slammed shut. I remember telling Payton, last time we went fishing, it was rough going through the inlet, and Alex did great getting us through it. I commented on my confidence in Alex's driving.

We were losing a lot of baitfish; they would flop out every time we hit a wave. Water kept spilling because the ocean did not smooth out like it did the last time. The previous trip was the only other time I had been out at sea, the only other time I had to compare this experience with! After we got through the inlet, we stopped and there were some adjustments made to the live well. We stopped every few minutes. Alex asked Patrick to put a bucketful of water into the live well. The water was still spilling out. I would say we did this at least ten times. Not only were we losing water and it was not recirculating in quick enough, we were losing a lot of our fish. Clearly, the guys thought this was a huge problem. The live well on this boat was located on the very back. We still had plenty of fish but didn't want to lose any more. Someone decided to engineer a way to keep the lid on and the fish from flopping out. Alex had a plastic grocery store bag that had been holding some snacks; he dumped them into the cooler. I had an extra hair tie around my wrist; I was instructed by someone to give it up. Alex did the deed and put the grocery bag around the piece in the live well that circulates water and tied the hair tie around it to hold it, and Patrick sat on it. This invention worked, and we continued out to sea!

It was a long ride out to the Tom Boyette Reef, and it wasn't really much smoother after we got past the inlet. Payton and I took the brand-new life jackets out of the cabin, took the plastic off, and used them for seat cushions. It seemed like we rode a really long way; still, we charged on into the deep blue sea. This seemed like much farther out than the last time we went fishing. Payton and I wondered, *How much farther? Are we almost there?* We were hoping we would soon slow down and troll, and not be slamming the waves so hard. We were hoping to lay out on the bow of the boat.

I recall Kenneth saying, "There are some really big swells."

I wondered, *Just how much farther are we going?* I looked back and thought to myself, *I can't see land,* but I wasn't truly panicked by this. I trusted my friends; more importantly, I trusted my future husband. We did not know a small craft warning had been issued since we left the dock, and Alex's boat absolutely met that criteria. None of our cell phones had service.

We were on the boat when Kenneth's dad texted him, "Don't go fishing today."

Finally, Alex announced that we had arrived at the reef! I never saw a buoy; it just looked like more open water. We slowed down and began to just go a few miles an hour while the guys were planning to begin to get the fishing gear and poles ready in the water to troll. We had been slowed down for a few seconds when we began to notice water from the live well spilling over the lip of the lid. We removed the hair tie and grocery bag. I do not remember who noticed the water spilling over or if it had been going on since we created the contraption. We had not paid the live well much attention after thinking the issue had been fixed. Water continued to spill over the lip of the live well. Water covered the floor in what seemed like seconds. Almost in sync with the spilling of the water, the engine screamed and squealed like it was chewing on something. It began to struggle; it was moaning, like it was about to give out.

Kenneth said to Alex, "I think we need to turn back," and Alex turned the boat immediately. I walked to the cocaptain's chair, leaned against Kenneth, and squeezed his arm. I remember him telling me, "It's going to be okay. We're going back." But, his face did not agree with what he was saying.

I cried out in my head, *Jesus!* I knew things were *not* okay. After Alex turned the boat, it was no longer taking waves by the nose. The waves were crashing toward the back of the boat. Starting to panic, in my heart and head, I began to cry out, *"Jesus! What do I do? Help us!"* The engine cut. In my spirit I knew I had to go under the cabin and get more life jackets. A wave crashed over the back of the boat; water poured into the boat! I immediately went under the cabin. The cabin was packed full of all kinds of things we thought we might need or want. I grabbed the life jackets and a throw cushion; there were two life jackets in my arms.

I will never forget the look on Payton's face as I turned, coming out of the cabin. She stood to my left, in the back corner of the boat. I threw her a life jacket and yelled, "Put it on now!" I saw Patrick in the back of the boat, to my right, using a sand bucket to shovel out the water. The waves crashed into the boat continually; the boat was thrashing around. Alex tried to crank the boat continually; it would not turn over. I had only grabbed two more life jackets—all I could easily grab in one swoop. All that were not stored under the bed. I realized I had to go back for another life jacket; there were five of us! At that moment, another wave crashed over the back of the boat, and the waves kept coming. The back of the boat was getting weighed down quickly. I put on a life jacket. Two more life jackets were lying on the floor of the boat, and none of the guys moved to put them on. I screamed for Kenneth to put one on. None of the guys listened and put the life jackets on! Alex made a Mayday call on his radio; there was no response. Alex attempted to call a few times. This transpired in a matter of seconds, I wouldn't even say minutes. He screamed into the radio; Alex's hand was shaking.

Payton then yelled, *"Will you jump with me?"* and offered me her hand. I threw off my tennis shoes, afraid they would weigh me down, and grabbed her hand. We jumped in.

Afraid that the suction of the boat would pull us under, I urged her to swim a few yards away with me. The only knowledge I had of boats sinking was from watching *Titanic* as a child. We squeezed each other's hands as tightly as we could. We got an entirely different view of the boat. Seeing the boat from floating in the ocean, we saw that the majority of what would normally be showing of Alex's boat was already underwater. I just knew the boat was about to roll over and completely sink.

With tears rolling down her face, Payton screamed and cried out hysterically, *"This is all your fault!"* I knew it was my fault she was out there; she had wanted to tan on the beach. I had talked her into coming.

Tears rolling down my face, I told her, "We have to pray!" I said, "Pray with me!" And we began to pray out loud to God.

It looked as if Kenneth, Alex, and Patrick were moving in slow motion. After treading water as hard as we could for maybe a minute, I had the thought, I left my phone on the boat! I yelled to Kenneth, *"Get a phone! Call 911!"* We had not done this before; we had only called Mayday. Kenneth grabbed his phone and Payton's phone, which were lying out in plain sight. Kenneth tried to call 911 while still standing on the boat, but there was no service. He grabbed a life jacket; he held it under his arm. Patrick put a life jacket on and did not move; he stood frozen. He had stopped shoveling water. Alex continued to try to call Mayday. He threw out a cooler and told Payton and me to hold on to it as another floating device.

Suddenly everything that was in the boat skidded to the back of the cockpit; it was horrific. The guys ran to the front part of the boat. Water poured and flooded over the back of the boat. The entire back half of the boat that was now underwater, and the nose was in the air. Alex threw the captain's throw cushion into the water. Payton and I held one hand, the cushion strap over our arms, and we each held one handle of the cooler. The nose of the boat was slowly going higher into the sky. Payton and I screamed with fear for the guys to jump in before they got caught under the boat.

The guys jumped. It seemed to happen in unison. As the guys jumped, the boat slammed over. Kenneth kept one of his arms over his head when he jumped in; he was able to keep the two phones above the water. He had the life jacket under his other arm. Those phones were now our only possible connections to land. The phones got splashed but not fully submerged. For a moment I panicked; Kenneth and Patrick were above water, but where was Alex? Was he stuck under the boat? *Finally*, he came up. *Probably* only ten seconds later, but in this situation, it seemed like forever.

Kenneth handed Payton her phone, which was in a water-resistant case. She began trying to call 911. We took turns trying to make the touch screen work with our fully soaking wet fingers, while the other would pray out loud. We tried to press numbers with our nose. We tried to use Siri, because the screen would not work with our wet fingers. After a while, her phone screen looked like a black-and-white TV channel that wouldn't come through. We could not get a callout. Her case hadn't worked; her phone was useless. Her phone had been damaged by the water. We threw her phone into the empty cooler we were using as a flotation device.

Payton cried out when she felt something touch her leg. I told her it was me. She screamed loudly, "I can see your feet! it wasn't you!" She began to talk about a biology class she had recently taken; she started to speak about sharks. I was wondering if the boat was going to completely sink and suck someone under, or if we would be able to use it as a floating device. Then, I forced myself to stop thinking about it; I reminded myself to pray.

Kenneth pulled himself on top of the part of the boat above water. He was hanging on to an upside-down boat while it was being pounded by waves, holding his arm in the air trying to get service. He curled his toes around the bar from the bow of the boat and supported his body weight by holding on to one of the ridges of the V-hull of the bottom of the bow. It looked like a balancing act. The waves threw him off many times, but he was strong. He kept pulling himself back onto the thrashing boat. Kenneth continually called 911. He could not get service, but he kept trying.

I tried to console Payton, and really myself too, with every Bible story I could remember, every verse I could quote. Every snippet of hope I could recall, the portions of Bible stories I knew. Even when I did not know who the people were really—I just knew the story in general. I began to pray out loud in the Spirit and told Payton, "We have to keep praying!"

A few of the specific prayers I remember are asking God to put a "force field" of angels around us like a hedge of protection, for God to bind out any creature of the sea that would attack us—we were over the artificial reef when the boat capsized. I asked God to calm the seas, and to send someone before dark. I began to thank God for sending someone. Payton prayed with me the entire time. I did not know I could pray this way, myself, until I did. I had no choice. If I stopped for a moment, Payton picked up. When she would stop, I would pick up. The majority of the time, we were both praying out loud as hard as we could.

I cried out to God, "Tell Linda to pray!" God had given Mrs. Linda the gift of the Holy Spirit. Her knowledge in the Spirit was way beyond any understanding. I cried out, "God, tell her to get on her face. Tell her to tell her church we need their prayers *now*!" It was Sunday morning. I prayed to God for her to have her congregation agree. In my spirit, I could feel God was sending someone, or maybe I just had to tell myself this at the time. I had some sort of supernatural peace that I now know could only have been from God. I kept telling Payton, "Someone is coming. God's not going to leave us out here to die. He has too many plans for us!" At that moment it hit me: it didn't matter that I had done my homework. I did not allow myself to go any further with that train of thought!

I started praying harder and louder. I'm sure if people could have seen me, they would have thought I was crazy. The people that were with me probably thought I was crazy, but I didn't care. Urgent prayer was our lifeline.

Alex was confused by what was going on, because most of our prayers were in the Spirit. We did not have the words. In the flesh, we knew we wouldn't last long. We could all look around and see each other; we had nothing. A few times, Alex asked if we were singing, which frustrated us, but we kept praying. We told him we were praying. Patrick clung to the front of the boat that was out of water; frozen, he did not speak. At some point, he put his life jacket on. Alex asked his brother if he put the plug in the boat. Patrick did not answer his brother. We had been on the water for a few hours that morning. I thought to myself, *Wouldn't we have sunk long before now if it was the plug?*

Alex saw a purple Rain Gatorade floating in the distance and swam away from us to get it. This frustrated me at first; I felt like he didn't realize how serious of a situation we were in. *We're floating in the middle of the ocean with what's left of an upside-down boat, four life jackets, a throw cushion, and a cooler. Screaming out prayers.* Kenneth desperately continued to call 911. Kenneth desperately continued to call 911 and hold himself on the V of the boat.

Alex swam back with the Gatorade and began to drink from it; then it hit me: conserve! I screamed at Alex not to drink a lot. Realizing we all might have to share that one Gatorade for a while, I was starting to feel dehydrated already. The waves kept crashing over our heads, soaking us, and the salt was drying us out. Nothing else floated up; that one Gatorade was all we had. Someone had taken it out of the cooler while we were riding out that morning; everything else was trapped under the boat, still in the other cooler.

Payton was wearing her watch. It was thirty-eight minutes before *Kenneth got service. He got service!* The waves must have been moving us fairly quickly. He told the 911 operator that we were over the Tom Boyette Reef when the boat capsized and that there were five people in the water. And he lost service. He continually repeated himself on the phone; Kenneth was screaming. He lost service again. We kept praying. He kept calling.

Kenneth did not know at this point that the iPhone my parents had gotten him and added to their business plan six days ago was water resistant. Nor did anyone. It was just the latest iPhone!

Payton and I stayed in prayer. Payton asked me a few more times, "Did you just touch my leg?" And when I answered yes, she would say, "No, you didn't. I can see your legs. That wasn't you!"

I would say, "We have to keep praying." There were little baitfish all around us. The baitfish did not want to leave the boat, it seemed.

After what seemed like a really long time of treading water, Payton and I decided the boat was going to stay partially afloat. We tried to crawl onto the V of the boat that was upside down. We helped each other as best as we could and continued to be thrown away by waves. I shoved Payton's butt up as hard as I could, trying to get her high enough on the boat so she would stay on. We both received cuts from our efforts, getting knocked off the boat hull by the rough water. Kenneth had plenty of cuts as well. We were exerting so much energy and only succeeded in falling off and getting cuts and bad rub burns. Payton asked me, "Why would God let us die out here? We're so young?"

I answered her, "We are going to bring some important things to the world. God is not going to let us die out here. We have so much potential!" I kept praying. Payton kept praying too. We were on top of a reef surrounded by baitfish; we were practically shark bait. I don't know if I actually saw a shark fin, or frightened myself into seeing something that resembled one. I did not dare to look again; I prayed.

I finally yelled to Kenneth, *"Call my dad!"* I could tell by the look on his face he knew this was the right thing to do, but he didn't want to. Finally, after trying to call him time after time, he got service and the call went through. My dad answered, just like he always does. I'm not exactly sure how their conversation went because I was screaming and praying out loud in the Spirit, praising God that Kenneth got a call through, and that Dad answered!

I remember hearing Kenneth say the words: "We're not going to make it, Mr. Don. This is it!" And I continued to yell scripture. My dad was panicked and sick on the other end of the line. He was hardly able to comprehend what he was being told. When he found out we were almost ten miles offshore, he was "pissed off" that we had gone out that far. He was remembering telling us that he thought Alex's boat was too old to be safe to go far. He instantly switched off that emotion, though, to one of trying to rescue us. When he said he was going to hang up and call for help, Kenneth would not let him hang up! Mr. Don, *you cannot hang up!*

My dad had been working a couple miles from home, on a "fix-er-upper," before church. Since Kenneth did not want to hang up, he had to get to another phone. Dad stayed on the line with Kenneth, praying and talking while he drove home from the Blueberry House. I can imagine my father driving as fast as he could to get to my mother. When Dad ran inside, he grabbed Mom's cell phone and the landline/house phone. First, he called 911 in Wayne County. They told him to call 911 in Pender County for Topsail Beach.

Mom had been in the shower, getting ready for church. Dad was shouting; she heard my father telling the 911 operator that our boat had capsized ten miles offshore. Mom. Could. Hardly. Breathe. As. She. Got. Out. Of. The. Shower. As she moved to her closet to pull clothes off hangers, she just kept repeating, *"Jesus!" "Jesus!"*

Kenneth continued to hold on to the boat, staying on the phone. He said it was the most intense workout of his life just to hold on. But God.

When Kenneth was telling my dad that we would not make it, I yelled at him, "I can do all things through Christ, who gives me strength."

Kenneth said to my dad, "They're not going to be able to find us by boat. It's too rough. They're going to have to come by air." Kenneth knew a family friend of ours had a small plane; he was hoping they could get it in the air.

Kenneth then thought to send my father a PIN of his current location! Dad could share our exact location with emergency services! Because we kept losing service every so often, we knew we were moving quickly in the water. Kenneth was repeatedly pinging our location. The 911 operator, on the phone with Dad, willingly gave my father her personal cell number so that he could share the pinged location with her. My dad would screenshot what Kenneth sent him and continually forward it to the 911 operator's personal cell. She, in turn, was sharing it with the US Coast Guard. Dad was on two phone lines with the 911 operator!

We would drift, and Kenneth would lose service. My dad would call him back. Kenneth told my dad, "It's the best feeling in the world to hear your voice on land. If we get disconnected, call me back."

Dad stayed on two or three phone lines, one to Pender County 911 and one with Kenneth, and when he had the chance, he would call someone to pray. Dad called Mrs. Linda, and she answered! On a Sunday morning during church. Never do I remember Mrs. Linda Burroughs having her phone on during church. While she was preaching, she answered a phone call! Right then, she asked the entire church to pray! Mrs. Linda prayed in the Spirit, on the phone with my Dad. Here is what God gave her for my father:

Trust in Me! For there is nothing that you can do! For this is in My hands (GOD). When this is over, son, remember everyone's life is always in My hands. And it is always a desperate situation, and they don't know it. Now, I have spoken calmness to your daughter (Brooke). I am supporting them, and they are in My hands. Keep trust in Me, says the Lord!

Linda said God had given *me* peace! My dad could not believe this, that in such a situation, I could have *peace*!

Meanwhile, my mom was facedown on the den floor, praying. Somewhere amid the frantic communications, they realized Mom needed to call Kenneth's parents. When she called Sharon's number, his parents were outside running. Hardly knowing what to say, Mom told Sharon that the Lord must have big plans for Brooke and Kenneth, and then spilled out what was happening in the Atlantic. Not thinking clearly, she asked the Freemans to come to my parents' house. Moments later, though, Dad decided it was time to head to Topsail Island. Mom called the Freemans back to adjust the plan; they would meet at the beach. As my dad furiously drove to Topsail Island, he called Payton's father. Dad told him about the emergency and asked him to use any connections he had to help! Perhaps there was a military connection? My parents kept two cell lines going, one with Kenneth and the other with emergency services or for calling family members.

The 911 operator told Dad that there was a plane in the air! A Coast Guard plane had been diverted from Elizabeth City, North Carolina.

About thirty minutes later, a plane with an American flag painted on its belly came soaring over! I recall waving my arms in the air and weeping hysterically. I cried out, *"Jesus!"* It didn't feel real. I cried uncontrollably, *"Thank You God!"* The plane continued to circle us and drop flares. Kenneth and my father lost service again and were not on the phone anymore for the remainder of the time we were in the water.

About ten minutes later, a US Coast Guard boat arrived. One by one, we were thrown a big flotation device to grab onto. I pushed Payton toward the bouy; she was pulled onto the boat first. I went right behind her. We were pulled onto a small USCG boat. They assessed our cuts and gave us water; it seemed like a blur. I remember kissing Kenneth, and Payton's forehead! I had never kissed Payton before, and maybe she thought that it was weird, but I was *praising God!* Payton started talking military with the Coast Guard guys. Her father, grandfather, uncle, oldest sister, and brother Dayton are all in, or have served in, the military.

Meanwhile, the 911 emergency operator called my dad to say that the Coast Guard was with us and that two of us were already on board, and that all five of us appeared to be okay!

We waited for a larger US Coast Guard boat to arrive so we could get onto it. They explained to us that the smaller boat could get to us faster but that the larger boat was safer to carry us back on. We jumped back into the ocean and grabbed a flotation device to be pulled onto the larger boat. Kenneth left his cell phone behind on the small boat since we were getting into the water again, not wanting to accidentally submerge it. Once we were all on the larger boat, we headed in, to the Wrightsville Beach Coast Guard Station.

As we left the capsized boat, we saw the towing company coming out to get Alex's boat! We witnessed just one old gentleman, by himself, jump off the skiff, into the water, and swim over and hook a rope to Alex's boat. He then proceeded to get back on his skiff and floor it. Alex's boat flipped right side up, and he towed it away in the opposite direction! It did not seem real. Did that man just snatch that boat right side up like that?

Using the personal phone of a Coast Guard personnel, I called my parents; they were just arriving at the beach. At some point, they had called Kenneth's parents. (The Meadows family had called Alex and Patrick's mother.) Dad said my cousin and her husband were at the Wrightsville Beach Coast Guard Station waiting for us. They had been at Topsail already and headed there to meet us since they could be there sooner.

Then I walked to the cockpit of the huge USCG boat and threw up. I was so emotional. I couldn't process everything that had just happened. I was in disbelief. I could not sit inside the boat cabin; it was so humid. I felt so emotionally sick. This is the moment it hit me. We should have died out there—BUT GOD. Then, I looked down. Written on a metal plate on the floor of the Coast Guard ship was the word FREEMAN. In two short weeks, this would be my last name. I called Kenneth over, not sure if I was hallucinating! He assured me it was really there! The Coast Guard crew was in disbelief as well. Kenneth agreed at this time that God had been with us the entire time!

Two Weeks Later

Thirteen days later, Kenneth and I said "I do" in front of all our families and friends. Our officiate even spoke about our "survival" story. Thank God we had a wedding and not a quintet funeral. *Thank You, God, for my miracle!*

More Than a Year Later

When I reflect on being in the ocean, I still cry thinking back about the supernatural strength and peace God gave to me that day while we were in the water. Only from God—it was not me! Looking back, I cannot believe it myself! My husband laughs at me because I cry when the silliest things bring a fierce memory back. I praise God! Looking back at that day, and the following days, doesn't even seem real; none of it does. I can vividly remember eating breakfast the next morning, weeping through the entire meal. We were back in Rosewood, at a local breakfast diner with my parents. I was in absolute disbelief of everything that had occurred in twenty-four hours.

These days, Payton is prepping for the DAT and hoping to go to dental school. I graduated with my MSW. Kenneth is working as a hog farmer and in school getting his MSW. We sadly lost touch with Patrick and Alex.

I believe prayer changes things. I was twenty-two years old when I was stranded in the ocean and cried out to God. I am a *survivor*. To God be the glory!

In loving memory of the men lost at sea,
just days before and after us.
God be with their families.

I have been asked hundreds of times in my life why God allows tragedy and suffering. I have to confess that I really do not know the answer totally, even to my own satisfaction. I have to accept, by faith, that God is sovereign, and He is a God of love and mercy and compassion in the midst of suffering.

—Billy Graham

Tom Boyette Reef AR-362

AR-362 is 8.7 nautical miles from New Topsail Inlet on a heading of 126 degrees. It is officially known as Tom Boyette Reef but locally known as "the first set of boxcars." The original material used to make the reef were train boxcars, thus the name. In 1992 and 2002, concrete pipes were added to the site. GPS coordinates location: 34° 15.717'/077° 30.450' (www.topsailangler.com). Note: A yellow buoy was removed in 2014 after GPS technology made it unnecessary (NC Onshore and Inshore Fishing, 2014).

References

Bishop, J. (2015, December 22). 55% of doctors have seen medical miracles & 74% believe in miracles. Retrieved from https//jamesbishopblog.wordpress.com/2015/12/22/55-of-doctors-have-seen-medical-miracles-74-believe&#8230

Chan, F. (2014, December 4). *Living eternally: The rope sermon* [Video file]. Retrieved from http//m.youtube.com/watch?v=bfvbH4Ugj7M

Holy Bible New Living Translation. (2015). Carol Stream, IL Tyndale House Publishers.

Strobel, L. (2018). *The case for miracles A journalist investigates evidence for the supernatural.* Zondervan. ISBN 0310259185.

About the Author

Brooke Neal Freeman is a young Christian outdoorswoman, newly married to the man God made for her. A clinical social worker and a beginning flower farmer/florist, Brooke is determined to share the story of her miracle. She experiences great joy seeing God's beauty in nature. She has learned to recognize the miracles in her life and seeks to honor her Lord with all she does. Brooke lives in Eastern North Carolina with her husband in an 1849 farmhouse across the road from Brooke's Fresh Cut Flower Farm.

CPSIA information can be obtained
at www.ICGtesting.com
Printed in the USA
LVHW090154300321
682929LV00008B/61